Great Whi

The Great White Shark is a very cool and a very scary undersea creature. This shark is just one of over 470 different species of the sharks living in the oceans today. These animals are closely related to the Stingray. Great White Sharks can grow to be very large. It is thought that these sharks have been around for about 350 million years. In this book we are going to explore the world of the Great White Shark. So sit back and be prepared to be wowed. Read on....

Where in the World?

Did you know the Great White Shark lives in water between 12 and 24 °C (54 and 75 °F)? The Great White Shark is very particular about the temperature of its water. It lives not far off shore in many places like, the east coast of the United States and also around South Africa and even Hawaii

Great White Shark

Curious Kids Press

The Body of the Great White Shark

Did you know the body of this shark is shaped like a torpedo? This fish is a highly feared predator. It has a pointed snout, 5 gill slits on its face and a crescent-shaped tail fin. It also has a pointed dorsal fin on its back and one fin on each side of its body. Sharks have a great sense of smell, hearing and eyesight.

The Size of a Great White Shark

Did you know the Great White Shark can grow to be huge? Believe it or not, the female shark is bigger than the male. Most Great Whites grow to be about 12 to 16 feet long (3.7 to 4.9 meters). They can weigh around 5,000 pounds (2,268 kilograms). The biggest great white shark on record was 23 feet long (7 meters). It weighed in at 7,000 pounds (3200 kilograms).

The Mouth of the Great White Shark

Did you know the mouth of the Great White Shark is very large? If you were to see a Great White swimming, its mouth does not look all that large. But when his great fish opens wide, its mouth is huge! This fish can eat a seal in a couple of chomps.

The Teeth of a Great White Shark

Did you know the Great White Shark has around 300 teeth? Perhaps the most ferocious thing about this shark is its sharp teeth. Each pointed tooth can measure more than 2.5 inches long (5.7 centimeters). Its teeth are arranged in rows and are used for giving a powerful bite.

The Skin of the Great White Shark

Did you know the Great White Shark is made of cartilage? This is like the end of our noses. The Great White is steel gray on top of its body, with white skin on its underbelly. This shark's skin is so rough that people have used it for sandpaper.

What the Great White Shark Eats

Did you know the Great White Shark is a carnivore? This means it only eats meat. This shark dines on sea mammals like seals and sea lions. They will also eat fish, smaller sharks and rays. The Great White Shark can eat a large meal, then not eat for weeks after.

How the Great White Shark Hunts

Did you know the Shark hunts using the element of surprise? When this shark sees a seal, it will quietly swim underneath it. Then in a burst of speed, it swims upwards and leaps out of the water. This is called, breaching. When the shark falls back into the water it most often has the seal in its mouth.

The Great White Shark Has a Special Ability

Did you know the Great White Shark can swim very fast? This type of shark can reach speeds of 43 miles-per-hour (69 kilometers-per-hour). It uses its powerful fins to achieve this speed. Also, the Great White has to swim constantly or it will sink to the bottom of the ocean.

Enemies of the Great White Shark

Did you know the Great White Shark has few enemies? Since this shark is so large it has few natural predators. Young Great Whites will be preyed upon by orcas. Sometimes the mother Great White will eat her own young, as well. Man has also hunted this shark.

Great White Shark Mom

Did you know the mother Great White does not have babies until she is 12 to 14 yearsold? The female Great White has eggs in her womb. These eggs hatch out inside of her. She can have from 2 to 10 baby sharks inside of her. Once the babies are born, the mother leaves them to survive on their own.

Baby Great White Sharks

Did you know the baby Great White Shark is called, a pup? The pups are already large at birth. Each little shark can measure 5 feet long (1.5 meters). Baby sharks look just like the adults do. The babies grow very quickly and will feed on fish and other small sea mammals.

Life of the Great White Shark

Did you know most Great White Sharks can live a very long time? This species of shark can live to be around 70 years-old! You can see Great White Sharks in some Marine exhibits. They are a fascinating fish that can be very scary, as well.

The Great White Shark and People

Did you know the Great White Shark does not want to eat people? Even though there has been some shark attacks, Great Whites would rather eat a seal. People have too many bones for the Great White to digest. Great Whites will "test bite" to see if their prey is yummy. This is how most people get bit.

Quiz

Question 1: How long has the Great White Shark been around?

Answer 1: About 350 million years

Question 2: What shape is the Great White Shark?

Answer 2: Torpedo-shaped

Question 3: What is special about the Great White Shark's mouth?

Answer 3: It has around 300 sharp pointed teeth

Question 4: What has shark skin been used for?

Answer 4: Sandpaper

Question 5: How many pups can a Great White Shark mom have?

Answer 5: From 2 to 10

Thank you for checking out another title from Curious Kids Press! Make sure to search "Curious Kids Press" on Amazon.com for many other great books.

CPSIA information can be obtained at www.ICGtesting.com
Printed in the USA
BVIW12n1635171215
430546BV00023B/61

* 9 7 8 1 4 9 7 5 1 7 6 9 1 *